MAKER OF THINGS

by

Denise Fleming

photographs by

Karen Bowers

Richard C. Owen Publishers, Inc.
Katonah, New York

Meet The Author

Richard C. Owen Publishers, Inc.
PO Box 585
Katonah, New York 10536

Library of Congress Cataloging-in-Publication Data

Fleming, Denise, 1950-
        Maker of things / by Denise Fleming ; photographs by Karen Bowers.
                p. cm. — (Meet the author)
        Summary: This writer and illustrator describes her life, her daily activities, and her creative process, showing how all are intertwined.
        ISBN 1-57274-596-7
        1. Fleming, Denise, 1950—-Juvenile literature. 2. Authors, American—20th century—Biography—Juvenile literature. 3. Children's literature—Authorship—Juvenile literature. [1. Fleming, Denise, 1950- 2. Authors, American. 3. Illustrators. 4. Women—Biography.] I. Bowers, Karen, ill. II. Title. III. Meet the author (Katonah, N.Y.)

PS3556.L438 Z469 2002
813'.54—dc21
[B]
                                                2002074268

Editorial, Art, and Production Director *Janice Boland*
Production Assistants *Donna Parsons* and *Elaine Kemp*
Administrative Assistance *Janet Lipareli*

Color separations by Leo P. Callahan, Inc., Binghamton, NY

Printed in the United States of America

9   8   7   6   5   4   3   2   1

To David, who makes all things possible

Dear Readers,

On January 31, 1950 I was born in Toledo, Ohio
to Frank and Inez Fleming. For almost five years
I was an only child. In December 1954,
my sister, Rochelle, was born.
That same year my grandparents gave me
a beautiful Siamese kitten named Abigail.

I was lucky enough to grow up in a neighborhood
full of kids. We were always busy. We spent the summers
sleeping out of doors, riding bikes, acting out stories,
and creating villages from great big cardboard boxes
that we dragged home from the appliance store.

The Sanger Branch Library was just a short bike ride away.
Once a week I'd visit the library and pick out three books to read.
I never imagined that years later, when the library
opened the doors of its new building, I would be leading my friends
and family on a tour of the Children's Room—
which was designed around my books.

I often spent weekends with my grandparents.
My father's mother was a great gardener.
She taught me all about the flowers and the creatures
that lived in her garden. As we ate breakfast, we would
watch the birds at the feeder and look them up in the bird guide.
Grandma raised hundreds of flowers called African violets.
I helped her root the cuttings and repot the plants.

My mother's mother had a garden of mostly tomato plants
behind her garage. When the tomatoes were ripe,
we'd take the saltshaker out to the garden, sit ourselves
down, and eat our fill of tomatoes. She'd tell stories
about her childhood and what it was like to grow up
as the oldest girl in a family of eleven children.
My grandmothers were total opposites in
personality, but both felt very strongly about
education and learning.

I liked school and did well grade-wise,
especially in English and art, but on almost every
report card there would be comments about my messy desk
and the fact that I spent too much time talking to classmates.
Some things never change—I still have a messy desk,
and at times I still talk too much.

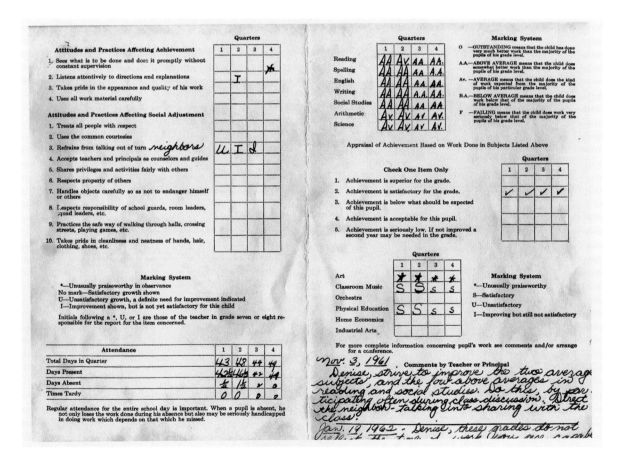

Every Saturday from third grade through eighth grade
I attended art classes at The Toledo Museum of Art.
Sometimes the instructors would hold classes in the galleries
where we studied different painters and their techniques.
The Impressionists were my favorites. I wanted to live
in their paintings. Before class my friends and I
would wander through the galleries, making up stories
to go with the paintings and sculptures.

My love of strong color was
inspired by my mother's
decorating. She filled our house
with brightly colored fabrics and
painted the walls
shades of deep green, yellow,
lavender, and coral.
She planted the gardens around
our house with masses of flowers.

My dad had a basement workshop where I spent hours
making things out of clay, wood, paint, wheat paste
and newspaper—whatever was available.

My husband David also likes to make things.
Together we've built furniture, rooms, stone walls,
and sculptures. If I had to give myself
a title it would be "Maker of Things."

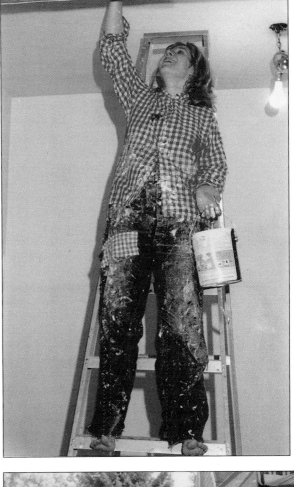

During high school I took lots of art classes,
but I never really thought about art as a career.
As graduation neared, I realized I had to choose something
to do. Since I liked art more than anything else,
I applied to Kendall School of Art and Design
in Grand Rapids, Michigan.

Kendall didn't offer any classes in book illustration.
But during art school I began to collect picture books
as a source of inspiration for my own artwork.
And it was in art school that I met my husband David.
He was an illustration major.

After art school I worked as a freelance artist.
It was years before I got up enough nerve to go
to New York City and look for book work.

There were books in my head that I wanted to share.
But I was always more comfortable making art than writing.
Writing has so many rules and I was worried
I'd make a mistake.

I decided I'd risk making mistakes and started to write.
I was forty-one when *In the Tall, Tall Grass* was published.
It was the first book I both wrote and illustrated.

When I get an idea, I rush to find a pencil and paper
so I can write my idea down before I forget it.
The handwriting on my first draft is large and sloppy
as I have to write quickly. I don't worry about spelling,
grammar, or punctuation on my first draft—
that all comes later.

What is important is the idea.
Sometimes I make little, scribble-drawings
in the margins, as I use illustrations to help tell my stories.

I read over my first draft and circle all the parts that I like.

Then I write a second draft, which I have my husband
or daughter read out loud. That helps me check
the rhythm and rhyme. If they stumble over a word
or phrase, I know I need to work on that area.
I write draft after draft. I can spend a whole day
moving one word around.

Even though most of my books have few words,
I start with hundreds of words. I write and rewrite
until I have just the right words to tell the story.
I keep a thesaurus and a rhyming dictionary
close at hand in case I need a bit of help.

I love language and rhythm and rhyme.
Some words just feel good in your mouth.
I collect words, phrases, and rhymes.

I have stacks of index cards with book ideas.
I even have titles for books that haven't been written yet.

Every now and then I have trouble making a story work.
Often, I'm unhappy with the ending.
I put the story away and don't look at it for a while.
When I take it out weeks or months later,
I can see exactly what I need to change
because now I'm looking at it with fresh eyes.

Sometimes ideas for books just appear.
One morning I was "lazing" in bed
when I thought I heard kittens mewing.
I went outside and found that a stray cat
had moved her litter of kittens to a place of safety
under our porch. The cat and her kittens were the
inspiration for my book *Mama Cat Has Three Kittens*.

Usually the words for my books come first,
but sometimes I see pictures and then add words.

A picture of a bear had been in my head for a while.
I like the solid shape of bears and I thought
I'd like to contrast the bulk of a bear with much smaller creatures.
I started sketching and then I began to think about the story.

One of the most interesting things
bears do is hibernate.
I researched hibernation and
found all sorts of other creatures
that sleep through the cold months
of the year. The bear in my head
became the bear in *Time to Sleep*.

22

Many of my books are about nature.
I can spend hours watching birds, insects,
and other creatures go about their lives.
My husband David, my daughter Indigo, and I
have planted our yard to be wildlife-friendly.
There are many plants that provide food for birds
and butterflies, a garden pond, and lots of trees
and bushes for shelter.

All sorts of creatures—bats, bees, bugs,
raccoons, possums, squirrels, box turtles, rabbits,
owls, frogs, fish, toads, snakes, woodchucks,
chipmunks, moles, shrews, and mice—live in our yard.
Occasionally, a skunk visits.

23

Quite a few animals have lived with us over the years: dogs, fish, cats, guinea pigs, mice, birds, rabbits, hamsters, and injured squirrels. For several years my daughter raised butterflies. We also have a horse named Erik who lives nearby at a stable. Recently two rats, Bella and Ruby, joined our family.

Many of these creatures have appeared in my books and, chances are, you will see some of them again in future books.

People often wonder how I make the pictures
for my books. I create them by a process called
pulp painting, a simple paper-making technique.

To create a pulp painting I make a mixture of water
and small, brightly-colored, cotton fibers.

This mixture of water and cotton fiber is called pulp.
I pour some of the pulp onto a wire screen.
The water drains through the screen.
The fiber stays on top of the screen
and forms the base and background
for my pulp painting.

For shapes with soft edges I "draw" on the background using squeeze bottles filled with colored pulp.

For shapes with hard edges I cut a stencil of the shape
out of a foam material similar to the foam meat trays
used at the supermarket. I place the stencil on the background
and pour brightly colored pulp into the stencil shape.

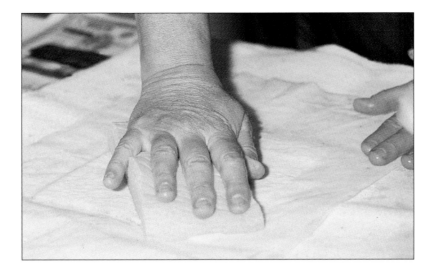

To create unusual textures I add all sorts of different materials
to the pulp such as coffee grounds, pine needles, or dried leaves.
I build up layer after layer of color and shape.
Once I have an image I am happy with,
I flip the sheet of wet fiber off the screen, press it, and dry it.

The result is — an image in handmade paper.

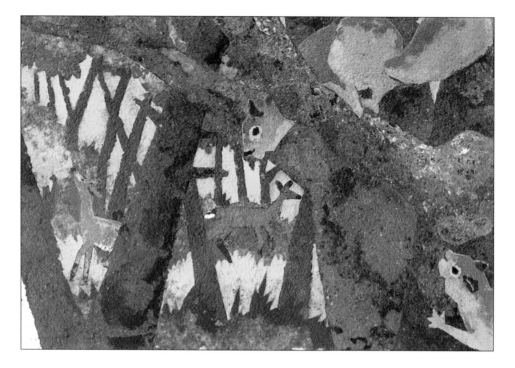

I can't imagine not making books.
Every time I put words and pictures together
to make a book it seems like magic.
I feel very lucky to be able to make a living
doing something that is so satisfying.

Your friend,

Denise Fleming

Denise Fleming

Other Books by Denise Fleming

Backyard Banter; Count; Lunch

About the Photographer

Karen Bowers is an award-winning
photographer. Her studio Shoot for the
Moon is in Toledo, Ohio, where she lives
with her four cats. Karen spent several days
with Denise Fleming taking the pictures for
this book. Karen told us it was a real
pleasure working on this project.

Acknowledgments

Illustration on page 3 from *In a Small, Small Pond* by Denise Fleming,
copyright ©1993 by Denise Fleming, reprinted by permission of Henry Holt
and Co., LLC. Illustration on page 21 from *Mama Cat Has Three Kittens* by
Denise Fleming, copyright ©1998 by Denise Fleming. Illustration on page
22 from *Time To Sleep* by Denise Fleming, copyright ©1997 by Denise
Fleming. Illustration on page 24 from *In the Tall, Tall Grass* by Denise
Fleming, copyright ©1991 by Denise Fleming. Illustration on page 30 from
Where Once There Was a Wood by Denise Fleming, copyright ©1996 by
Denise Fleming. Reprinted by permission of Henry Holt and Company,
LLC. Impressionist paintings on page 9 *The Dance Class* by Edgar Degas,
The Bridge at Villeneuve-la-Garenne by Alfred Sisley.

Meet the Author titles

Verna Aardema *A Bookworm Who Hatched*
David A. Adler *My Writing Day*
Frank Asch *One Man Show*
Joseph Bruchac *Seeing the Circle*
Eve Bunting *Once Upon a Time*
Lynne Cherry *Making a Difference in the World*
Lois Ehlert *Under My Nose*
Denise Fleming *Maker of Things*
Jean Fritz *Surprising Myself*
Paul Goble *Hau Kola Hello Friend*
Ruth Heller *Fine Lines*
Lee Bennett Hopkins *The Writing Bug*
James Howe *Playing with Words*
Johanna Hurwitz *A Dream Come True*
Karla Kuskin *Thoughts, Pictures, and Words*
Thomas Locker *The Man Who Paints Nature*
Jonathan London *Tell Me a Story*
George Ella Lyon *A Wordful Child*
Margaret Mahy *My Mysterious World*
Rafe Martin *A Storyteller's Story*
Patricia McKissack *Can You Imagine?*
Laura Numeroff *If You Give an Author a Pencil*
Patricia Polacco *Firetalking*
Laurence Pringle *Nature! Wild and Wonderful*
Cynthia Rylant *Best Wishes*
Seymour Simon *From Paper Airplanes to Outer Space*
Mike Thaler *Imagination*
Jean Van Leeuwen *Growing Ideas*
Jane Yolen *A Letter from Phoenix Farm*

For more information about the Meet the Author books
visit our website at www.RCOwen.com or call 1-800-336-5588

Date Due

OCT 26 07			
MAR 3 1 2012			

BRODART   Cat. No. 23 233   Printed in U.S.A.